PRAYER JOURNAL

A Woman After God's Own Heart

Reflections from

ELIZABETH GEORGE

[handwritten inscription:] To Laura — as we pray faithfully you are blessed to have Cindy as your friend. Elizabeth George 1-23-99

HARVEST HOUSE PUBLISHERS
Eugene, Oregon 97402

Cover by Garborg Design Works, Minneapolis, Minnesota

A WOMAN AFTER GOD'S OWN HEART PRAYER JOURNAL
Copyright © 1999 by Elizabeth George
Published by Harvest House Publishers
Eugene, Oregon 97402

ISBN 0-7369-0060-8

Printed in the United States of America.

99 00 01 02 03 04 / DH / 10 9 8 7 6 5 4 3 2 1

An Invitation to Prayer

⌒

Imagine living life so that people thought of each of us—today and long after we're gone—as a woman after God's own heart! Our transformation into a woman after God's own heart is indeed God's work. But it is also the fruit of the soul that desires, cultivates, and nurtures such a heart!

This prayer journal, dear follower of God, is a focus on one discipline—the discipline of prayer—that helps us to place ourselves before God so that He can do His transforming work of grace in our lives. Each day you'll find practical insights and prayers that will help you follow after God in every area of life and cultivate an impassioned relationship with Him. I welcome you to join me in seeking to become the woman God calls you and will empower you to be: a woman after God's own heart.

The Blessings of Prayer

My own journey into prayer began when I dared to pray this prayer on my tenth spiritual birthday: "Lord, what do You see missing from my Christian life? What needs attention as I begin a new decade with You?" God seemed to respond immediately by calling to my mind an area of great personal struggle and failure: my prayer life!

Oh, I had tried praying. But each new effort lasted, at best, only a few days. I would set aside time for God, read my Bible, and then dutifully bow my head, only to mumble a few general words which basically added up to, "God, please bless my family and me today." Certainly God intended prayer to be more than that, but I couldn't seem to do it.

3

On that spiritual birthday, I reached for a small book of blank pages and began a prayer journal. My new commitment to prayer put into motion a complete make-over of my whole life—every part and pursuit of it. Initially, I expected prayer to be drudgery and joyless labor. But oh, the many blessings that blossomed in my life proved otherwise! I was genuinely surprised—and overjoyed!—at how prayer was changing me, the world around me, and my walk with God.

Why do I encourage you, too, to pray? Because of these (and many more!) blessings:

- Prayer increases faith.
- Prayer provides a place to unload burdens.
- Prayer teaches us that God is always near.
- Prayer trains us not to panic.
- Prayer changes lives.
- Prayer leads us to greater purity.
- Prayer gives us a confidence in making decisions.
- Prayer helps to improve relationships.
- Prayer brings contentment.
- Prayer produces the ministry of prayer.

The Path to Prayer

How can we cultivate a heart of prayer and enjoy the blessings that accompany a life of committed and devoted prayer? How can we begin our journey on the path to prayer? Here are some simple steps you can take . . . today:

- Start a prayer journal to record your requests and responses as you make your own personal journey of prayer.
- Set aside some time each day to linger with the Lord in prayer, and remember that *something is better than nothing.* Begin small—and watch for the mighty effects!
- Pray always (Ephesians 6:18) and in all places, enjoying God's presence with you wherever you go (Joshua 1:9).
- Pray faithfully for others—including your enemies (Matthew 5:44)! Take seriously the powerful privilege of the ministry of prayer.

4

A Plan for Prayer

What exactly should you pray about? Let me share some ideas by describing how I created the plan that became this prayer journal—a plan for praying and practicing God's priorities each day as a woman after God's own heart. I began by focusing on the following areas:

> *God*—First, when considering your relationship with God, pray, "Lord, what can I do today to live out the fact that You are the ultimate priority of my life and that I am truly a woman after Your own heart?" Write down God's answers and promptings to this matter of the heart.
>
> *Husband*—If you are married, pray, "God, what can I do today to let my husband (be sure you use his name!) know he is most important to me next to You?" I would encourage you to jot down God's direction. If you are not married, pray similarly regarding your parents, family members, and best friends.
>
> *Children*—Do you have children (and grandchildren)? Pray, "Lord, what can I do today for these precious gifts from You? (Don't forget to use their names!) How can I let them know that, after my husband, they are more important than all the other people in my life? How can I show each of them my love?"
>
> *Home*—Praying about homemaking lifts it out of the physical realm and transports it into the spiritual. So pray something like, "Lord, what can I do today regarding my home? What can I do today to make our home a little bit of heaven, our own 'home, sweet home'?"
>
> *Self*—Lay your life before God and pray, "Lord, what can I do today to grow spiritually? In what specific ways can I prepare for future ministry?"
>
> *Ministry*—Continue on with, "Lord, what can I do today to minister to Your people?" Because this is usually a long list, whisper another prayer and ask God to help you prioritize it.
>
> *Others*—Finish up your time of prayer with, "And, Lord, what else would You have me do today?"

These heart-cries, dear friend, put your feet—and heart!—on the pathway to further becoming a woman after God's own heart. Your answers each day will differ as God points to various attitudes and actions He wants added to and eliminated from your life as you follow Him. After all, your longing is to be a woman after God's own heart—a woman who purposes to do His will (Acts 13:22).

The Journey of Prayer

And now it's time to begin. It's fun to talk about prayer and easy to think about prayer, but it's time to pray! Take pen in hand and purpose to pray, using this prayer journal. Fill your heart and soul with prayer. Fill these pages with the outpourings of your heart. Make yours a life of prayer!

My personal growth

_____

_____

_____

_____

My ministry

_____

_____

_____

_____

My other heart concerns

_____

_____

_____

_____

My heart response

_____

_____

_____

_____

A woman after God's heart is a woman who prays. Her heart naturally overflows in prayer as well as in caring. And since praying for people is a powerful way to care for them, you and I will want to join with God in a ministry of prayer—a ministry that makes a huge difference in people's lives.

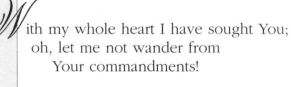

ith my whole heart I have sought You;
oh, let me not wander from
Your commandments!

—PSALM 119:10

My relationship with God

_____

_____

_____

_____

My husband/family

_____

_____

_____

_____

My children/friends

_____

_____

_____

_____

My home

_____

_____

_____

_____

My personal growth

_____
_____
_____
_____

My ministry

_____
_____
_____
_____

My other heart concerns

_____
_____
_____
_____

My heart response

_____
_____
_____
_____

Lord, help me to seek Your ways in all things.

*A*s you therefore have received Christ Jesus the Lord, so walk in Him, rooted and built up in Him and established in the faith.

—COLOSSIANS 2:6,7

The root of the righteous yields fruit.

—PROVERBS 12:12

My relationship with God

_____
_____
_____
_____

My husband/family

_____
_____
_____
_____

My children/friends

_____
_____
_____
_____

My home

_____
_____
_____
_____

My personal growth

_____
_____
_____
_____

My ministry

_____
_____
_____
_____

My other heart concerns

_____
_____
_____
_____

My heart response

_____
_____
_____
_____

The health of anything—whether a garden plant or a heart devoted to God—reflects on what is going on (or not going on) underground. If God is going to be first in our heart and the ultimate priority of our life, we must develop a root system anchored deep in Him.

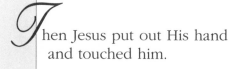

*hen Jesus put out His hand
and touched him.*

—MATTHEW 8:3

My relationship with God

_____
_____
_____
_____

My husband/family

_____
_____
_____
_____

My children/friends

_____
_____
_____
_____

My home

_____
_____
_____
_____

My personal growth

_____
_____
_____
_____

My ministry

_____
_____
_____
_____

My other heart concerns

_____
_____
_____
_____

My heart response

_____
_____
_____
_____

*W*hen it comes to reaching out, remember this principle of ministry: Your very presence is a source of comfort. You may not have the exact words to say or the perfect Scripture to share. But in many (if not most) situations, your touch can bring comfort far greater than words.

Date_____

A s He was praying in a certain place,
when He ceased . . . one of His
disciples said to Him, "Lord,
teach us to pray."

—LUKE 11:1

My relationship with God

_____
_____
_____
_____

My husband/family

_____
_____
_____
_____

My children/friends

_____
_____
_____
_____

My home

_____
_____
_____
_____

My personal growth

_____
_____
_____
_____

My ministry

_____
_____
_____
_____

My other heart concerns

_____
_____
_____
_____

My heart response

_____
_____
_____
_____

*P*rayer isn't easy! It's definitely a discipline, but it's also a ministry that flows from a full heart. Three decisions can help you place yourself before God so He can fill your heart with concern for others: Determine a time, determine a place, determine a plan.

I beseech you therefore, brethren, by the mercies of God, that you present your bodies a living sacrifice, holy, acceptable to God, which is your reasonable service . . . that you may prove what is that good and acceptable and perfect will of God.

—ROMANS 12:1,2

My relationship with God

_____
_____
_____
_____

My husband/family

_____
_____
_____
_____

My children/friends

_____
_____
_____
_____

My home

_____
_____
_____
_____

My personal growth

_____
_____
_____
_____

My ministry

_____
_____
_____
_____

My other heart concerns

_____
_____
_____
_____

My heart response

_____
_____
_____
_____

*E*very morning, in a heartfelt prayer either written or silent, start fresh with God. Lord, I give You all that I am, all that I have . . . now . . . forever . . . and daily lay everything and everyone in my life on Your altar.

That you may become blameless and harmless, children of God without fault in the midst of a crooked and perverse generation, among whom you shine as lights in the world.

—PHILIPPIANS 2:15

My relationship with God

_____
_____
_____
_____

My husband/family

_____
_____
_____
_____

My children/friends

_____
_____
_____
_____

My home

_____
_____
_____
_____

My personal growth

_____
_____
_____
_____

My ministry

_____
_____
_____
_____

My other heart concerns

_____
_____
_____
_____

My heart response

_____
_____
_____
_____

If we faithfully nurture what is beneath the surface of our life, people will marvel at what they see of God in us!

Date_____

*F*ear not, for I am with you; be not dismayed, for I am your God. I will strengthen you, yes, I will help you, I will uphold you with My righteous right hand.

—ISAIAH 41:10

My relationship with God

_____
_____
_____
_____

My husband/family

_____
_____
_____
_____

My children/friends

_____
_____
_____
_____

My home

_____
_____
_____

My personal growth

_____
_____
_____
_____

My ministry

_____
_____
_____
_____

My other heart concerns

_____
_____
_____
_____

My heart response

_____
_____
_____
_____

*L*ord, away from the world and hidden from public view, I exchange my weariness for Your strength, my weakness for Your power, my darkness for Your light, my problems for Your solutions, my burdens for Your freedom, my frustrations for Your peace, my turmoil for Your calm, my hopes for Your promises, my afflictions for Your balm of comfort, my questions for Your answers, my confusion for Your knowledge, my doubt for Your assurance, my nothingness for Your awesomeness, the temporal for the eternal, and the impossible for the possible.

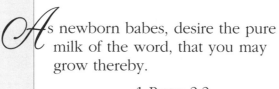

As newborn babes, desire the pure milk of the word, that you may grow thereby.

—1 PETER 2:2

My relationship with God

_____
_____
_____
_____

My husband/family

_____
_____
_____
_____

My children/friends

_____
_____
_____
_____

My home

_____
_____
_____
_____

My personal growth

_____

_____

_____

_____

My ministry

_____

_____

_____

_____

My other heart concerns

_____

_____

_____

_____

My heart response

_____

_____

_____

_____

*O*nly through consistent exposure to God's Word can we draw out the nutrition needed to grow a heart of faith.

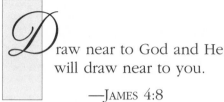

raw near to God and He
will draw near to you.

—JAMES 4:8

My relationship with God

_____

_____

_____

_____

My husband/family

_____

_____

_____

_____

My children/friends

_____

_____

_____

_____

My home

_____

_____

_____

_____

My personal growth

_____

_____

_____

_____

_____

My ministry

_____

_____

_____

_____

_____

My other heart concerns

_____

_____

_____

_____

My heart response

_____

_____

_____

_____

_____

*D*eveloping the habit of drawing near to God definitely helps make our devotional life what we need it to be, and what God wants it to be.

earch me, O God, and know
my heart; try me, and know
my anxieties.

—PSALM 139:23

My relationship with God

_____
_____
_____
_____

My husband/family

_____
_____
_____
_____

My children/friends

_____
_____
_____
_____

My home

_____
_____
_____
_____

My personal growth

_____

My ministry

_____

My other heart concerns

_____

My heart response

_____

ecoming pure is a process of spiritual growth, and taking seriously the confession of sin during prayer time moves that process along, causing us to purge our life of practices that displease God.

*T*he Lord is my strength and my shield; my heart trusted in Him, and I am helped.

—PSALM 28:7

My relationship with God

_____

_____

_____

_____

My husband/family

_____

_____

_____

_____

My children/friends

_____

_____

_____

_____

My home

_____

_____

_____

_____

My personal growth

_____
_____
_____
_____

My ministry

_____
_____
_____
_____

My other heart concerns

_____
_____
_____
_____

My heart response

_____
_____
_____
_____

When we spend time with Christ,
He supplies us with strength and
encourages us in the pursuit
of His ways.

*W*e do not look at the things which are seen, but at the things which are not seen. For the things which are seen are temporary, but the things which are not seen are eternal.

—2 Corinthians 4:18

My relationship with God

_____
_____
_____
_____

My husband/family

_____
_____
_____
_____

My children/friends

_____
_____
_____
_____

My home

_____
_____
_____
_____

My personal growth

_____
_____
_____
_____

My ministry

_____
_____
_____
_____

My other heart concerns

_____
_____
_____
_____

My heart response

_____
_____
_____
_____

*I*magine what kind of transformation would occur in our hearts if we spent time (or more time) each day drawing near to God through His Word—time spent on something of eternal, life-changing value!

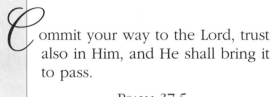

ommit your way to the Lord, trust also in Him, and He shall bring it to pass.

—PSALM 37:5

My relationship with God

_____
_____
_____
_____

My husband/family

_____
_____
_____
_____

My children/friends

_____
_____
_____
_____

My home

_____
_____
_____
_____

My personal growth

_____

_____

_____

_____

My ministry

_____

_____

_____

_____

My other heart concerns

_____

_____

_____

_____

My heart response

_____

_____

_____

_____

*O*ur devotion to God is strengthened when we offer Him a fresh commitment each day.

I am the vine, you are the branches. He
who abides in Me, and I in him, bears
much fruit; for without Me you can
do nothing.
—JOHN 15:5

My relationship with God

_____
_____
_____
_____

My husband/family

_____
_____
_____
_____

My children/friends

_____
_____
_____
_____

My home

_____
_____
_____
_____

My personal growth

_____
_____
_____
_____

My ministry

_____
_____
_____
_____

My other heart concerns

_____
_____
_____
_____

My heart response

_____
_____
_____
_____

> The impact of our ministry to people will be in direct proportion to the time we spend away from people and with God.

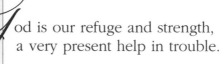

od is our refuge and strength,
a very present help in trouble.

—PSALM 46:1

My relationship with God

_____
_____
_____
_____

My husband/family

_____
_____
_____
_____

My children/friends

_____
_____
_____
_____

My home

_____
_____
_____
_____

My personal growth

_____
_____
_____
_____

My ministry

_____
_____
_____
_____

My other heart concerns

_____
_____
_____
_____

My heart response

_____
_____
_____
_____

The more we pray, the more we will realize the fact of God's omnipresence, the reality that He is always present with His people, including me and you! Cultivating a heart of prayer is a sure way to experience God's presence.

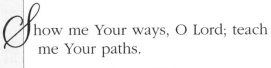 how me Your ways, O Lord; teach
me Your paths.

—PSALM 25:4

My relationship with God

_____

_____

_____

_____

My husband/family

_____

_____

_____

_____

My children/friends

_____

_____

_____

_____

My home

_____

_____

_____

My personal growth

_____
_____
_____
_____

My ministry

_____
_____
_____
_____

My other heart concerns

_____
_____
_____
_____

My heart response

_____
_____
_____
_____

*M*ake no decision without prayer.

I say to you, love your enemies, bless those who curse you, do good to those who hate you, and pray for those who spitefully use you and persecute you.

—MATTHEW 5:44

My relationship with God

_____
_____
_____
_____

My husband/family

_____
_____
_____
_____

My children/friends

_____
_____
_____
_____

My home

_____
_____
_____
_____

My personal growth

_____
_____
_____

My ministry

_____
_____
_____

My other heart concerns

_____
_____
_____

My heart response

_____
_____
_____
_____

*J*esus instructed us to pray for our enemies, and God changes our hearts as we do so.

*B*lessed is the man who trusts in the Lord, and whose hope is the Lord. For he shall be like a tree planted by the waters, which spreads out its roots by the river, and will not fear when heat comes; but its leaf will be green, and will not be anxious in the year of drought, nor will cease from yielding fruit.

—JEREMIAH 17:7,8

My relationship with God

_____
_____
_____
_____

My husband/family

_____
_____
_____
_____

My children/friends

_____
_____
_____
_____

My home

_____
_____
_____
_____

My personal growth

_____
_____
_____
_____

My ministry

_____
_____
_____
_____

My other heart concerns

_____
_____
_____
_____

My heart response

_____
_____
_____
_____

A's you and I regularly draw needed refreshment from God's Word, He creates in us a reservoir of hope and strength in Him. Then, when times are rough, we won't be depleted. We won't dry up, disintegrate, or die. Instead, we will simply reach down into our hidden reservoir of refreshment and draw out what we need from what God has given us.

I have not departed from the commandment of His lips; I have treasured the words of His mouth more than my necessary food.

—JOB 23:12

My relationship with God

_____
_____
_____
_____

My husband/family

_____
_____
_____
_____

My children/friends

_____
_____
_____
_____

My home

_____
_____
_____
_____

My personal growth

_____
_____
_____
_____

My ministry

_____
_____
_____
_____

My other heart concerns

_____
_____
_____
_____

My heart response

_____
_____
_____
_____

urely drawing near to God's Word should be of utmost importance to us each day! We discover great joy when we grow to love it more than food for our bodies.

et each of you look out not only for his own interests, but also for the interests of others.

—PHILIPPIANS 2:4

My relationship with God

_____
_____
_____
_____

My husband/family

_____
_____
_____
_____

My children/friends

_____
_____
_____
_____

My home

_____
_____
_____
_____

My personal growth

_____
_____
_____
_____

My ministry

_____
_____
_____
_____

My other heart concerns

_____
_____
_____
_____

My heart response

_____
_____
_____
_____

As you and I settle our personal needs with God in private prayer, we can then rise up and focus all our attention outward—away from self and onto others.

lessed are those who keep His
testimonies, who seek Him with the
whole heart!

—PSALM 119:2

My relationship with God

_____
_____
_____
_____

My husband/family

_____
_____
_____
_____

My children/friends

_____
_____
_____
_____

My home

_____
_____
_____
_____

My personal growth

_____
_____
_____
_____
_____

My ministry

_____
_____
_____
_____
_____

My other heart concerns

_____
_____
_____
_____
_____

My heart response

_____
_____
_____
_____
_____

As for godly or personal endeavors, God will reveal them to us and their order of priority when we pray, search the Scriptures, and seek wise counsel. He will show us how to be women after His heart in every detail of our lives.

*T*he Lord will be your confidence.
—PROVERBS 3:26

My relationship with God

_____
_____
_____
_____

My husband/family

_____
_____
_____
_____

My children/friends

_____
_____
_____
_____

My home

_____
_____
_____
_____

My personal growth

_____
_____
_____
_____

My ministry

_____
_____
_____
_____

My other heart concerns

_____
_____
_____
_____

My heart response

_____
_____
_____
_____

God-confidence comes as the Holy Spirit works in us. As we pray and when we make choices that honor God, the Holy Spirit fills us with His power for ministry. When we are filled with God's goodness, we are confidently and effectively able to share His love and joy.

*T*he Son of Man did not come to be served, but to serve, and to give His life a ransom for many.

—MATTHEW 20:28

My relationship with God

_____
_____
_____
_____

My husband/family

_____
_____
_____
_____

My children/friends

_____
_____
_____
_____

My home

_____
_____
_____

My personal growth

_____
_____
_____
_____

My ministry

_____
_____
_____

My other heart concerns

_____
_____
_____
_____

My heart response

_____
_____
_____
_____

*B*eing a servant is a sign of Christian maturity; it is the true mark of Christ.

*T*he spirit of a man is the lamp of the LORD, searching all the inner depths of his heart.

—PROVERBS 20:27

My relationship with God

_____
_____
_____
_____

My husband/family

_____
_____
_____
_____

My children/friends

_____
_____
_____
_____

My home

_____
_____
_____

My personal growth

_____

_____

_____

_____

My ministry

_____

_____

_____

_____

My other heart concerns

_____

_____

_____

_____

My heart response

_____

_____

_____

_____

_____

> *L*ord, if there is any wrong way in my
> life, please call my attention to it. I
> know that to do anything contrary to
> Your will is to give You less than my whole heart.
> Help me to be responsive to You in all that I do.

*H*umble yourselves under the mighty hand of God, that He may exalt you in due time.

—1 Peter 5:6

My relationship with God

_____

_____

_____

_____

My husband/family

_____

_____

_____

_____

My children/friends

_____

_____

_____

_____

My home

_____

_____

_____

My personal growth

_____
_____
_____
_____

My ministry

_____
_____
_____
_____

My other heart concerns

_____
_____
_____
_____

My heart response

_____
_____
_____
_____

Lord, help me to desire all that You desire, love all that You love, and humble myself under Your mighty hand. Give me a heart that longs for You.

*D*o not worry about tomorrow, for tomorrow will worry about its own things. Sufficient for the day is its own trouble.

—MATTHEW 6:34

My relationship with God

_____

_____

_____

_____

My husband/family

_____

_____

_____

_____

My children/friends

_____

_____

_____

_____

My home

_____

_____

_____

_____

My personal growth

_____
_____
_____
_____

My ministry

_____
_____
_____
_____

My other heart concerns

_____
_____
_____
_____

My heart response

_____
_____
_____
_____

*A*ll God asks of you and me is to handle today, only today.

*Y*ou shall receive power when the
Holy Spirit has come upon you;
and you shall be witnesses to Me in
Jerusalem, and in all Judea and
Samaria, and to the end of the earth.

—Acts 1:8

My relationship with God

_____
_____
_____
_____

My husband/family

_____
_____
_____
_____

My children/friends

_____
_____
_____
_____

My home

_____
_____
_____
_____

My personal growth

_____
_____
_____
_____

My ministry

_____
_____
_____
_____

My other heart concerns

_____
_____
_____
_____

My heart response

_____
_____
_____
_____

Can you imagine having the power of God at work in your life? When Christ is your Savior, that's what happens: God empowers you through His Holy Spirit to do good, to effect change in your life, to make your life count, to help others, and to minister for Christ.

*I*f any of you lacks wisdom, let him ask of God, who gives to all liberally and without reproach, and it will be given to him.

—JAMES 1:5

My relationship with God

_____
_____
_____
_____

My husband/family

_____
_____
_____
_____

My children/friends

_____
_____
_____
_____

My home

_____
_____
_____
_____

My personal growth

_____
_____
_____
_____

My ministry

_____
_____
_____
_____

My other heart concerns

_____
_____
_____
_____

My heart response

_____
_____
_____
_____

*L*ord, give me a greater desire to serve You and others. Fill me with Your wisdom as I make decisions on where and how to minister.

*T*each me Your way, O Lord; I will walk in Your truth; unite my heart to fear Your name.

—PSALM 86:11

My relationship with God

_____
_____
_____
_____

My husband/family

_____
_____
_____
_____

My children/friends

_____
_____
_____
_____

My home

_____
_____
_____

My personal growth

_____
_____
_____
_____

My ministry

_____
_____
_____
_____

My other heart concerns

_____
_____
_____
_____

My heart response

_____
_____
_____
_____

*O*bedience is a foundational stepping-stone on the path of God's will—the path we'll be following as women after His heart. Sure footing in this area of our lives will prepare us to respond to God's desire for how we live.

*H*e shall be like a tree planted by the rivers of water, that brings forth its fruit in its season, whose leaf also shall not wither; and whatever he does shall prosper.

—PSALM 1:3

My relationship with God

_____
_____
_____
_____

My husband/family

_____
_____
_____
_____

My children/friends

_____
_____
_____
_____

My home

_____
_____
_____
_____

My personal growth

_____
_____
_____
_____

My ministry

_____
_____
_____
_____

My other heart concerns

_____
_____
_____
_____

My heart response

_____
_____
_____
_____

*J*ust like a plant with its roots hidden underground, you and I—out of public view and alone with God—are to draw from Him all that we need to live the abundant life He has promised His children.

ast all your care upon Him, for He cares for you.

—1 Peter 5:7

My relationship with God

_____
_____
_____
_____

My husband/family

_____
_____
_____
_____

My children/friends

_____
_____
_____
_____

My home

_____
_____
_____
_____

My personal growth

_____
_____
_____
_____

My ministry

_____
_____
_____
_____

My other heart concerns

_____
_____
_____
_____

My heart response

_____
_____
_____
_____

*L*ingering in God's presence will increase our faith, provide a place for us to unload our burdens, remind us that God is always near, and help us not to panic. Prayer is one way God has provided for us to commune with Him, and when we accept His invitation to commune with Him, He will transform our hearts and change our lives.

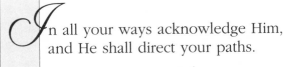

*I*n all your ways acknowledge Him,
and He shall direct your paths.
—PROVERBS 3:6

My relationship with God

_____
_____
_____
_____

My husband/family

_____
_____
_____
_____

My children/friends

_____
_____
_____
_____

My home

_____
_____
_____
_____

My personal growth

_____
_____
_____
_____

My ministry

_____
_____
_____
_____

My other heart concerns

_____
_____
_____
_____

My heart response

_____
_____
_____
_____

When we practice the principle of
making no decision without prayer,
we experience a divine assurance
with every step we take.

*W*e all, with unveiled face, beholding as in a mirror the glory of the Lord, are being transformed into the same image from glory to glory, just as by the Spirit of the Lord.

—2 CORINTHIANS 3:18

My relationship with God

_____
_____
_____
_____

My husband/family

_____
_____
_____
_____

My children/friends

_____
_____
_____
_____

My home

_____
_____
_____
_____

My personal growth

_____
_____
_____
_____
_____

My ministry

_____
_____
_____
_____
_____

My other heart concerns

_____
_____
_____
_____
_____

My heart response

_____
_____
_____
_____
_____

> *A* commitment to prayer can put into motion a complete make-over of your whole life—every part and pursuit of it.

*T*each us to number our days, that we may gain a heart of wisdom.

—PSALM 90:12

My relationship with God

_____

_____

_____

_____

My husband/family

_____

_____

_____

_____

My children/friends

_____

_____

_____

_____

My home

_____

_____

_____

_____

My personal growth

_____
_____
_____
_____

My ministry

_____
_____
_____
_____

My other heart concerns

_____
_____
_____
_____

My heart response

_____
_____
_____
_____

*E*ach day is important in and of itself because . . .

- What you are today is what you are becoming.
- You are today what you have been becoming.
- Every day is a little life, and our whole life is but a day repeated.

*K*eep your heart with all diligence,
for out of it spring the issues
of life.

—PROVERBS 4:23

My relationship with God

_____
_____
_____
_____

My husband/family

_____
_____
_____
_____

My children/friends

_____
_____
_____
_____

My home

_____
_____
_____
_____

My personal growth

_____
_____
_____
_____

My ministry

_____
_____
_____
_____

My other heart concerns

_____
_____
_____
_____

My heart response

_____
_____
_____
_____

The key, God says, to living a life of obedience—a life that stays on His path—is the heart. . . . If we keep our heart, if we diligently attend to it and guard it, then all of the issues, the actions, the "on-goings and the out-goings" of life will be handled God's way.

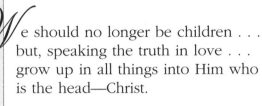

e should no longer be children . . .
but, speaking the truth in love . . .
grow up in all things into Him who
is the head—Christ.

—EPHESIANS 4:14,15

My relationship with God

_____
_____
_____
_____

My husband/family

_____
_____
_____
_____

My children/friends

_____
_____
_____
_____

My home

_____
_____
_____
_____

My personal growth

_____
_____
_____
_____

My ministry

_____
_____
_____
_____

My other heart concerns

_____
_____
_____
_____

My heart response

_____
_____
_____
_____

I have learned what it is that keeps us fresh and excited and motivated in our godly pursuits, and that is spiritual growth. Our spiritual growth in Jesus Christ—growing to be more like Him—strengthens our heart, fills it, and empowers us to obey His commands.

*S*ee then that you walk circumspectly,
not as fools but as wise, redeeming
the time, because the days are evil.
—EPHESIANS 5:15,16

My relationship with God

_____
_____
_____
_____

My husband/family

_____
_____
_____
_____

My children/friends

_____
_____
_____
_____

My home

_____
_____
_____
_____

My personal growth

_____

_____

_____

_____

My ministry

_____

_____

_____

_____

My other heart concerns

_____

_____

_____

_____

My heart response

_____

_____

_____

_____

*H*ow much is a minute worth? It's priceless or worthless, depending on how you use it.

*T*he wise woman builds her house, but the foolish pulls it down with her hands.

—PROVERBS 14:1

My relationship with God

_____

_____

_____

_____

My husband/family

_____

_____

_____

_____

My children/friends

_____

_____

_____

_____

My home

_____

_____

_____

_____

My personal growth

_____
_____
_____
_____

My ministry

_____
_____
_____
_____

My other heart concerns

_____
_____
_____
_____

My heart response

_____
_____
_____
_____

*L*ord, help me to weave a tapestry of beauty in my home, to speak words of encouragement and hope to family and friends.

*O*h, the depth of the riches both of the wisdom and knowledge of God! How unsearchable are His judgments and His ways past finding out!

—ROMANS 11:33

My relationship with God

_____
_____
_____
_____

My husband/family

_____
_____
_____
_____

My children/friends

_____
_____
_____
_____

My home

_____
_____
_____
_____

My personal growth

_____

_____

_____

_____

My ministry

_____

_____

_____

_____

My other heart concerns

_____

_____

_____

_____

My heart response

_____

_____

_____

_____

*I*ncreasing in knowledge is a lot like getting the evening meal on the table. We have to have a plan. Begin to develop a plan for increasing in knowledge, remembering that something is better than nothing. The important thing is to do something.

You shall love the Lord your God
with all your heart, with all your soul,
with all your strength, and with all
your mind, and your neighbor
as yourself.

—LUKE 10:27

My relationship with God

_____
_____
_____
_____

My husband/family

_____
_____
_____
_____

My children/friends

_____
_____
_____
_____

My home

_____
_____
_____
_____

My personal growth

_____

_____

_____

_____

My ministry

_____

_____

_____

_____

My other heart concerns

_____

_____

_____

_____

My heart response

_____

_____

_____

_____

God calls us to love Him, first and foremost, with all our heart, soul, strength, and mind and to allow that rich love we enjoy in Him to overflow into our neighbors, into the lives of others. That's why a heart strengthened by spiritual growth in Him is so very important.

*T*o this end I also labor, striving according to His working which works in me mightily.

—COLOSSIANS 1:29

My relationship with God

_____
_____
_____
_____

My husband/family

_____
_____
_____
_____

My children/friends

_____
_____
_____
_____

My home

_____
_____
_____
_____

My personal growth

_____
_____
_____
_____
_____

My ministry

_____
_____
_____
_____
_____

My other heart concerns

_____
_____
_____
_____

My heart response

_____
_____
_____
_____
_____

God is responsible for presenting the opportunities to minister—in His time, place, and manner—but we are responsible for cooperating with His efforts to prepare us.

*M*y grace is sufficient for you, for My strength is made perfect in weakness." Therefore most gladly I will rather boast in my infirmities, that the power of Christ may rest upon me. . . . For when I am weak, then I am strong.

—2 CORINTHIANS 12:9,10

My relationship with God

_____
_____
_____
_____

My husband/family

_____
_____
_____
_____

My children/friends

_____
_____
_____
_____

My home

_____
_____
_____
_____

My personal growth

_____
_____
_____
_____

My ministry

_____
_____
_____
_____

My other heart concerns

_____
_____
_____
_____

My heart response

_____
_____
_____
_____

*N*o matter what the problem, the hurdle, the struggle, the suffering you face, God promises, "My grace is sufficient for you." Whether you're dealing with temptation, a difficult marriage, problems with the children, needs in the home, personal challenges, a stretching ministry, or any other difficult situation, God promises, "My grace is sufficient for you."

ommit your works to the Lord, and your thoughts will be established.

—PROVERBS 16:3

My relationship with God

_____

_____

_____

_____

My husband/family

_____

_____

_____

_____

My children/friends

_____

_____

_____

_____

My home

_____

_____

_____

_____

My personal growth

_____
_____
_____
_____

My ministry

_____
_____
_____
_____

My other heart concerns

_____
_____
_____
_____

My heart response

_____
_____
_____
_____

*G*oals provide focus. It's very true that if you aim at nothing, you'll hit it every time! . . . Setting goals that are specific help you move forward in the direction you want to go.

*B*lessed be the God and Father of our
Lord Jesus Christ, who has blessed us
with every spiritual blessing in the
heavenly places in Christ.

—EPHESIANS 1:3

My relationship with God

_____
_____
_____
_____

My husband/family

_____
_____
_____
_____

My children/friends

_____
_____
_____
_____

My home

_____
_____
_____
_____

My personal growth

_____
_____
_____
_____

My ministry

_____
_____
_____
_____

My other heart concerns

_____
_____
_____
_____

My heart response

_____
_____
_____
_____

As Christian women, you and I are filled with all spiritual blessings. Lord, help me to share the spiritual blessings You've given me with others and to invest my life in other hearts. Thank You for the precious gift of Your unconditional love.

*L*et the word of Christ dwell in you
richly in all wisdom, teaching and
admonishing one another in psalms
and hymns and spiritual songs,
singing with grace in your hearts
to the Lord.

—COLOSSIANS 3:16

My relationship with God

_____
_____
_____
_____

My husband/family

_____
_____
_____
_____

My children/friends

_____
_____
_____
_____

My home

_____
_____
_____
_____

My personal growth

_____
_____
_____
_____

My ministry

_____
_____
_____
_____

My other heart concerns

_____
_____
_____
_____

My heart response

_____
_____
_____
_____

> You cannot give away what you do not possess. A life of involvement in loving service and ministry to others requires that you be a full vessel.

*T*hose who wait on the Lord shall
renew their strength; they shall mount
up with wings like eagles.

—ISAIAH 40:31

My relationship with God

_____
_____
_____
_____

My husband/family

_____
_____
_____
_____

My children/friends

_____
_____
_____
_____

My home

_____
_____
_____
_____

My personal growth

_____
_____
_____
_____

My ministry

_____
_____
_____
_____

My other heart concerns

_____
_____
_____
_____

My heart response

_____
_____
_____
_____

The time we spend in solitude with our Bible and our prayer list, our secret life spent with our heavenly Father, is time spent waiting upon the Lord. Then, in the fullness of time, in God's perfect timing, there is the mounting up, the taking flight like an eagle. We are able to soar because we've been with the Lord.

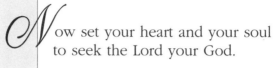

ow set your heart and your soul
to seek the Lord your God.

—1 CHRONICLES 22:19

My relationship with God

_____

_____

_____

_____

My husband/family

_____

_____

_____

_____

My children/friends

_____

_____

_____

_____

My home

_____

_____

_____

_____

My personal growth

_____
_____
_____
_____

My ministry

_____
_____
_____
_____

My other heart concerns

_____
_____
_____
_____

My heart response

_____
_____
_____
_____
_____

*R*everence for God is a must for a woman after God's heart!

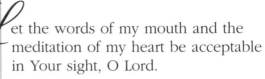

*L*et the words of my mouth and the meditation of my heart be acceptable in Your sight, O Lord.

—PSALM 19:14

My relationship with God

_____
_____
_____
_____

My husband/family

_____
_____
_____
_____

My children/friends

_____
_____
_____
_____

My home

_____
_____
_____
_____

My personal growth

_____
_____
_____
_____

My ministry

_____
_____
_____
_____

My other heart concerns

_____
_____
_____
_____

My heart response

_____
_____
_____
_____

*I*f you are faithful to commit to memory selected gems from God's Word, you'll suddenly find them adding real substance to your conversations.

*T*he older women likewise . . . be reverent in behavior, not slanderers, not given to much wine, teachers of good things.

—TITUS 2:3

My relationship with God

_____
_____
_____
_____

My husband/family

_____
_____
_____
_____

My children/friends

_____
_____
_____
_____

My home

_____
_____
_____
_____

My personal growth

_____
_____
_____
_____

My ministry

_____
_____
_____
_____

My other heart concerns

_____
_____
_____
_____

My heart response

_____
_____
_____
_____

By living out godliness you will teach and disciple many women—without saying a word! The best way to teach godliness to others is to model it.

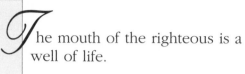

he mouth of the righteous is a well of life.

—PROVERBS 10:11

My relationship with God

_____
_____
_____
_____

My husband/family

_____
_____
_____
_____

My children/friends

_____
_____
_____
_____

My home

_____
_____
_____
_____

My personal growth

_____
_____
_____
_____

My ministry

_____
_____
_____
_____
_____

My other heart concerns

_____
_____
_____
_____
_____

My heart response

_____
_____
_____
_____
_____

*L*ord, give me a watchful concern for Your people. Use me to refresh many souls in need of encouragement, just like a rain cloud delivers much-needed moisture to a parched earth.

he opens her mouth with wisdom,
and on her tongue is the law
of kindness.

—PROVERBS 31:26

My relationship with God

_____
_____
_____
_____

My husband/family

_____
_____
_____
_____

My children/friends

_____
_____
_____
_____

My home

_____
_____
_____
_____

My personal growth

_____
_____
_____
_____
_____

My ministry

_____
_____
_____
_____
_____

My other heart concerns

_____
_____
_____
_____
_____

My heart response

_____
_____
_____
_____
_____

*R*elationships with people are enhanced when we follow in the steps of the Proverbs 31 woman, who opens her mouth with wisdom and kindness. If her thoughts weren't wise or kind, her mouth was shut!

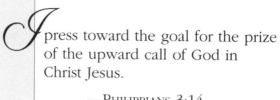

I press toward the goal for the prize of the upward call of God in Christ Jesus.

—PHILIPPIANS 3:14

My relationship with God

_____
_____
_____
_____

My husband/family

_____
_____
_____
_____

My children/friends

_____
_____
_____
_____

My home

_____
_____
_____
_____

My personal growth

_____
_____
_____
_____

My ministry

_____
_____
_____
_____

My other heart concerns

_____
_____
_____
_____

My heart response

_____
_____
_____
_____

*J*ust as goals help us in day-to-day life, they are definitely an aid when it comes to our spiritual growth. For me, goals provide a target. As I rise each morning and take aim at my day, the arrow I shoot may wobble and weave, but at least it's in flight and headed somewhere!

*T*est all things; hold fast what is good. Abstain from every form of evil. Now may the God of peace Himself sanctify you completely; and may your whole spirit, soul, and body be preserved blameless at the coming of our Lord Jesus Christ.

—1 THESSALONIANS 5:21-23

My relationship with God

_____

_____

_____

_____

My husband/family

_____

_____

_____

_____

My children/friends

_____

_____

_____

_____

My home

_____

_____

_____

_____

My personal growth

_____

My ministry

_____

My other heart concerns

_____

My heart response

_____

*A*re you purposefully filling your mind with knowledge of God's Word—knowledge you can give away to others? And does your body belong to God, to be groomed, cared for, and disciplined for maximum usefulness and His glory? And are you nurturing love for others—thinking, speaking, and acting toward them as Christ would?

*B*rethren, I do not count myself to have apprehended; but one thing I do, forgetting those things which are behind and reaching forward to those things which are ahead, I press toward the goal for the prize of the upward call of God in Christ Jesus.

—PHILIPPIANS 3:13,14

My relationship with God

_____

_____

_____

_____

My husband/family

_____

_____

_____

_____

My children/friends

_____

_____

_____

_____

My home

_____

_____

_____

_____

My personal growth

_____
_____
_____
_____

My ministry

_____
_____
_____
_____

My other heart concerns

_____
_____
_____
_____

My heart response

_____
_____
_____
_____

*O*nce we've acknowledged and dealt with our failure to follow God wholeheartedly, once we've addressed our acts of disobedience, you and I are to forget those things from the past and go on. Oh, we are to remember the lessons learned, but we train our heart to obey by following this command from God to press on!

*T*herefore, my beloved brethren, be steadfast, immovable, always abounding in the work of the Lord, knowing that your labor is not in vain in the Lord.

—1 Corinthians 15:58

My relationship with God

_____

_____

_____

_____

My husband/family

_____

_____

_____

_____

My children/friends

_____

_____

_____

_____

My home

_____

_____

_____

_____

My personal growth

_____
_____
_____
_____

My ministry

_____
_____
_____
_____

My other heart concerns

_____
_____
_____
_____

My heart response

_____
_____
_____
_____

*M*ay you know beyond all doubt that your labor for the Lord is never in vain. And may you never grow weary of doing good!

*L*ord, make me to know my end,
and what is the measure of my days,
that I may know how frail I am.

—PSALM 39:4

My relationship with God

_____

_____

_____

_____

My husband/family

_____

_____

_____

_____

My children/friends

_____

_____

_____

_____

My home

_____

_____

_____

_____

My personal growth

_____

_____

_____

_____

My ministry

_____

_____

_____

_____

My other heart concerns

_____

_____

_____

_____

My heart response

_____

_____

_____

_____

What you are today (based on choices you're making) is what you are becoming, and you are today what you have been becoming (based on choices you've already made). Our choices, which reflect our life standards, will determine whether or not we fulfill God's design for our life. Whether you are dealing with the next five minutes, the next hour, tomorrow, or forever, the choices you make are making all the difference in the world!

*D*o not let your beauty be that
outward adorning . . . but let it
be the hidden person of the heart,
with the incorruptible [beauty]
of a gentle and quiet spirit, which
is very precious in the sight of God.

—1 PETER 3:3,4

My relationship with God

_____
_____
_____
_____

My husband/family

_____
_____
_____
_____

My children/friends

_____
_____
_____
_____

My home

_____
_____
_____
_____

My personal growth

_____
_____
_____
_____

My ministry

_____
_____
_____
_____

My other heart concerns

_____
_____
_____
_____

My heart response

_____
_____
_____
_____

> *E*very morning remember that your goal is simple: You want to have just one good day of living for God. Stay focused on following God's plan for your life for just this one day. For just one day, put on His precious adornment of a gentle and quiet spirit. Put first things first.

he plans of the diligent lead surely to plenty.

—PROVERBS 21:5

My relationship with God

_____
_____
_____
_____

My husband/family

_____
_____
_____
_____

My children/friends

_____
_____
_____
_____

My home

_____
_____
_____

My personal growth

_____

_____

_____

_____

My ministry

_____

_____

_____

_____

My other heart concerns

_____

_____

_____

_____

My heart response

_____

_____

_____

_____

When my time of prayer and scheduling is over, I hold in my hand a master plan for the day—a plan that reflects my priorities, a plan that enables me to be the woman after God's own heart that I desire to be! Wisdom always has a plan.

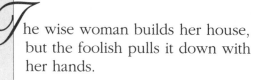

The wise woman builds her house, but the foolish pulls it down with her hands.

—PROVERBS 14:1

My relationship with God

_____

_____

_____

_____

My husband/family

_____

_____

_____

_____

My children/friends

_____

_____

_____

_____

My home

_____

_____

_____

_____

My personal growth

_____
_____
_____
_____

My ministry

_____
_____
_____
_____

My other heart concerns

_____
_____
_____
_____

My heart response

_____
_____
_____
_____

In this single verse God gives us wisdom for a lifetime. Decide to put away any destructive habits which are pulling down and destroying the little bit of heaven you are trying to build for others, and replace them with habits that ensure the completion of your work of art: your home and your family.

*D*elight yourself also in the Lord,
and He shall give you the desires
of your heart.

—PSALM 37:4

My relationship with God

_____
_____
_____
_____

My husband/family

_____
_____
_____
_____

My children/friends

_____
_____
_____
_____

My home

_____
_____
_____
_____

My personal growth

_____

_____

_____

_____

My ministry

_____

_____

_____

_____

My other heart concerns

_____

_____

_____

_____

My heart response

_____

_____

_____

_____

_____

*L*ord, perform open-heart surgery in me. Open my heart and fill it with Your desires for my life, and give me the strength and passion to fulfill those desires.

*B*e kindly affectionate to one another with brotherly love, in honor giving preference to one another.

—ROMANS 12:10

My relationship with God

_____
_____
_____
_____

My husband/family

_____
_____
_____
_____

My children/friends

_____
_____
_____
_____

My home

_____
_____
_____
_____

My personal growth

_____
_____
_____
_____

My ministry

_____
_____
_____
_____

My other heart concerns

_____
_____
_____
_____

My heart response

_____
_____
_____
_____

*O*ut of honor for God, we can give preference to other people in our lives. Our dedication to honoring people honors God and brings a beauty to our lives that reflects a heart after God.

*T*he heart of him who has understanding seeks knowledge, but the mouth of fools feeds on foolishness.

—PROVERBS 15:14

My relationship with God

_____
_____
_____
_____

My husband/family

_____
_____
_____
_____

My children/friends

_____
_____
_____
_____

My home

_____
_____
_____

My personal growth

_____
_____
_____
_____

My ministry

_____
_____
_____
_____

My other heart concerns

_____
_____
_____
_____

My heart response

_____
_____
_____
_____

Lord, help me to seek knowledge and guard against spending precious time on things that have no value.

*H*e who dwells in the secret place
of the Most High shall abide under
the shadow of the Almighty.

—PSALM 91:1

My relationship with God

_____
_____
_____
_____

My husband/family

_____
_____
_____
_____

My children/friends

_____
_____
_____
_____

My home

_____
_____
_____
_____

My personal growth

_____
_____
_____
_____

My ministry

_____
_____
_____
_____

My other heart concerns

_____
_____
_____
_____

My heart response

_____
_____
_____
_____

God's perspective on time is different from ours, and we may question His use of it. We may be tempted to think that quiet, hidden time with Him doesn't count—that it doesn't show, it doesn't matter, and no one cares. After all, nobody sees it! There's no glory, no splash, no attention given to those weeks, months, years of waiting on God. No one sees us read and study God's empowering Word; no one is present to watch us memorize and meditate on God's life-changing truths. God alone sees us on bended knee in the heart-wrenching work of prayer—work which He uses to prepare us for life and ministry.

*M*y heart is steadfast, O God, my heart is steadfast. . . . There is none upon earth that I desire besides You.

—PSALM 57:7; 73:25

My relationship with God

_____
_____
_____
_____

My husband/family

_____
_____
_____
_____

My children/friends

_____
_____
_____
_____

My home

_____
_____
_____
_____

My personal growth

_____
_____
_____
_____

My ministry

_____
_____
_____
_____

My other heart concerns

_____
_____
_____
_____

My heart response

_____
_____
_____
_____

Our heart for God should be like a boiling teakettle. Our heart should be characterized by God-given and intense emotion and passion for our Lord. When a teakettle is boiling on your stove, you know it! It sputters and steams and hops, empowered by its violent heat. Likewise, we should be fiery and excited about God, and time with God Himself will fuel that fire.

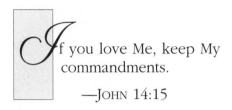

If you love Me, keep My
commandments.
—JOHN 14:15

My relationship with God

_____

_____

_____

_____

My husband/family

_____

_____

_____

_____

My children/friends

_____

_____

_____

_____

My home

_____

_____

_____

_____

My personal growth

_____

My ministry

_____

My other heart concerns

_____

My heart response

_____

A heart committed to doing God's will is an important ingredient when it comes to living out our love for God.

*I*f anyone is in Christ, he is a new creation; old things have passed away; behold, all things have become new.

—2 CORINTHIANS 5:17

My relationship with God

_____
_____
_____
_____

My husband/family

_____
_____
_____
_____

My children/friends

_____
_____
_____
_____

My home

_____
_____
_____
_____

My personal growth

_____
_____
_____
_____

My ministry

_____
_____
_____
_____

My other heart concerns

_____
_____
_____
_____

My heart response

_____
_____
_____
_____

> When you and I come to a saving knowledge of Jesus Christ, we are given a new beginning, a fresh start, forgiveness for the past, wisdom for handling life, and power for doing what's right.

he counsel of the Lord stands forever,
the plans of His heart to all generations.

—Psalm 33:11

My relationship with God

_____
_____
_____
_____

My husband/family

_____
_____
_____
_____

My children/friends

_____
_____
_____
_____

My home

_____
_____
_____
_____

My personal growth

_____
_____
_____
_____

My ministry

_____
_____
_____
_____

My other heart concerns

_____
_____
_____
_____

My heart response

_____
_____
_____
_____

*O*ur life situation may change, but God's Word never changes.

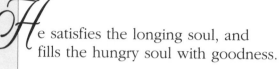

He satisfies the longing soul, and
fills the hungry soul with goodness.

—PSALM 107:9

My relationship with God

_____
_____
_____
_____

My husband/family

_____
_____
_____
_____

My children/friends

_____
_____
_____
_____

My home

_____
_____
_____
_____

My personal growth

_____
_____
_____
_____

My ministry

_____
_____
_____
_____

My other heart concerns

_____
_____
_____
_____

My heart response

_____
_____
_____
_____

t the end of each focused, quality day, your heart is satisfied and content. You have done the giving, the living, the following, and the loving. In return, God satisfied your longing heart and filled your hungry soul with His goodness. The peace that you sense is the satisfaction that comes from gladly being spent in doing God's will for just one day. Now . . . let that one day—that one step—encourage you to string your daily pearls of living out God's priorities into a lifetime of living as a woman after God's own heart!

esus answered and said to her, "Martha, Martha, you are worried and troubled about many things. But one thing is needed, and Mary has chosen that good part, which will not be taken away from her."

—LUKE 10:41,42

My relationship with God

_____

_____

_____

_____

My husband/family

_____

_____

_____

_____

My children/friends

_____

_____

_____

_____

My home

_____

_____

_____

_____

My personal growth

_____
_____
_____
_____

My ministry

_____
_____
_____
_____

My other heart concerns

_____
_____
_____
_____

My heart response

_____
_____
_____
_____

A woman after God's own heart chooses the one thing necessary for each day: She chooses to love God, worship God, walk with God, serve God, and look forward to being with Him in eternity.

> *D*o not worry about your life. . . .
> But seek first the kingdom of God
> and His righteousness, and all these
> things shall be added to you.
>
> —MATTHEW 6:25,33

My relationship with God

_____

_____

_____

_____

My husband/family

_____

_____

_____

_____

My children/friends

_____

_____

_____

_____

My home

_____

_____

_____

My personal growth

_____
_____
_____
_____

My ministry

_____
_____
_____
_____

My other heart concerns

_____
_____
_____
_____

My heart response

_____
_____
_____
_____

A daily prayer of commitment helps us to release what we think are our rights.

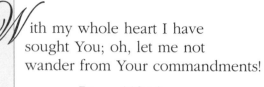

ith my whole heart I have
sought You; oh, let me not
wander from Your commandments!

—PSALM 119:10

My relationship with God

_____
_____
_____
_____

My husband/family

_____
_____
_____
_____

My children/friends

_____
_____
_____
_____

My home

_____
_____
_____
_____

My personal growth

_____
_____
_____
_____

My ministry

_____
_____
_____
_____

My other heart concerns

_____
_____
_____
_____

My heart response

_____
_____
_____
_____

A wholehearted love for God looks to Him through His Word and prayer, always watching and waiting, ever ready to do all that He says, prepared to act on His expressed desires. Such a heart—tender and teachable—will concentrate on doing what is right.

Date_____

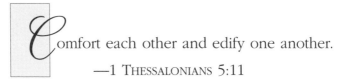

Comfort each other and edify one another.
—1 Thessalonians 5:11

My relationship with God

_____
_____
_____
_____

My husband/family

_____
_____
_____
_____

My children/friends

_____
_____
_____
_____

My home

_____
_____
_____
_____

My personal growth

_____
_____
_____
_____

My ministry

_____
_____
_____
_____

My other heart concerns

_____
_____
_____
_____

My heart response

_____
_____
_____
_____

*E*veryone needs edification and encouragement, and we are free to offer that when we have a heart filled by God.

*G*od . . . has saved us and called us
with a holy calling, not according to
our works, but according to His own
purpose and grace which was given
to us in Christ Jesus before time began.

—2 TIMOTHY 1:8,9

My relationship with God

_____
_____
_____
_____

My husband/family

_____
_____
_____
_____

My children/friends

_____
_____
_____
_____

My home

_____
_____
_____

My personal growth

_____
_____
_____
_____

My ministry

_____
_____
_____
_____

My other heart concerns

_____
_____
_____
_____

My heart response

_____
_____
_____
_____

*K*nowing what you are called to do by God, and choosing to wear the right hat at the right time, keeps you fully focused on the most important thing at hand at any given minute.

*W*hatever things are true, whatever things are noble, whatever things are just, whatever things are pure, whatever things are lovely, whatever things are of good report, if there is any virtue and if there is anything praiseworthy–meditate on these things.

—PHILIPPIANS 4:8

My relationship with God

_____
_____
_____
_____

My husband/family

_____
_____
_____
_____

My children/friends

_____
_____
_____
_____

My home

_____
_____
_____
_____

My personal growth

_____
_____
_____
_____

My ministry

_____
_____
_____
_____

My other heart concerns

_____
_____
_____
_____

My heart response

_____
_____
_____
_____

Thoughts that are critical, negative, harmful, and jealous not only go against God's Word, but they also spawn actions that are critical, negative, harmful, and jealous. So ask God to help you think loving, positive, sweet thoughts when it comes to other people.

Date_____

he extends her hand to the poor,
yes, she reaches out her hands to
the needy.

—PROVERBS 31:20

My relationship with God

_____
_____
_____
_____

My husband/family

_____
_____
_____
_____

My children/friends

_____
_____
_____
_____

My home

_____
_____
_____
_____

My personal growth

_____
_____
_____
_____

My ministry

_____
_____
_____
_____

My other heart concerns

_____
_____
_____
_____

My heart response

_____
_____
_____
_____

Lord help me to use the firstfruits of my free time to be filled spiritually so that I can serve You and Your people.

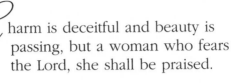

*C*harm is deceitful and beauty is passing, but a woman who fears the Lord, she shall be praised.

—PROVERBS 31:30

My relationship with God

_____
_____
_____
_____

My husband/family

_____
_____
_____
_____

My children/friends

_____
_____
_____
_____

My home

_____
_____
_____
_____

My personal growth

_____
_____
_____
_____

My ministry

_____
_____
_____
_____

My other heart concerns

_____
_____
_____
_____

My heart response

_____
_____
_____
_____

*I*n His power and by His grace, we keep following after God's heart—no matter what!

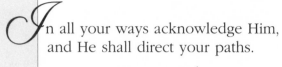

In all your ways acknowledge Him,
and He shall direct your paths.

—PROVERBS 3:6

My relationship with God

_____
_____
_____
_____

My husband/family

_____
_____
_____
_____

My children/friends

_____
_____
_____
_____

My home

_____
_____
_____
_____

My personal growth

_____
_____
_____
_____

My ministry

_____
_____
_____
_____

My other heart concerns

_____
_____
_____
_____

My heart response

_____
_____
_____
_____

Today's verse describes a two-step partnership with God: Our part is to stop and acknowledge God along the way, and His part is to direct our paths. We are to consult with God regarding every decision, word, thought, or response. Before we move ahead or merely react, we need to stop and pray first, "God, what would You have me do (or think or say) here?"

*P*raying always with all prayer and supplication in the Spirit, being watchful to this end with all perseverance and supplication for all the saints.

—Ephesians 6:18

My relationship with God

_____
_____
_____
_____

My husband/family

_____
_____
_____
_____

My children/friends

_____
_____
_____
_____

My home

_____
_____
_____
_____

My personal growth

_____
_____
_____
_____

My ministry

_____
_____
_____
_____

My other heart concerns

_____
_____
_____
_____

My heart response

_____
_____
_____
_____

As we invest ourselves in prayer for other people, we find ourselves wonderfully involved in their lives.

*B*lessed are those who keep
His testimonies, who seek Him
with the whole heart!

—PSALM 119:2

My relationship with God

_____
_____
_____
_____

My husband/family

_____
_____
_____
_____

My children/friends

_____
_____
_____
_____

My home

_____
_____
_____
_____

My personal growth

_____
_____
_____
_____

My ministry

_____
_____
_____
_____

My other heart concerns

_____
_____
_____
_____

My heart response

_____
_____
_____
_____

God will honor the time we commit to learning more about Him, the time we find, redeem, save, allow, and schedule for our spiritual growth.

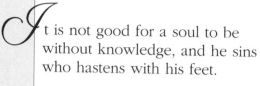

It is not good for a soul to be without knowledge, and he sins who hastens with his feet.

—PROVERBS 19:2

My relationship with God

_____
_____
_____
_____

My husband/family

_____
_____
_____
_____

My children/friends

_____
_____
_____
_____

My home

_____
_____
_____
_____